AT

Padel Excellence:

Integrating Psychology for Peak Performance

Auguste Torres

© Auguste Torres 2024

All rights reserved. No part of this publication may be reproduced, distributed, or transmitted in any form or by any means, including photocopying, recording, or other electronic or mechanical methods, without the prior written permission of the publisher, except in the case of brief quotations embodied in critical reviews and certain other non-commercial uses permitted by copyright law.

This book is designed to provide information on the subjects covered. It is sold with the understanding that the author and publisher are not engaged in rendering psychological, financial, legal, or other professional services. If expert assistance is needed, the services of a competent professional should be sought.

The author and publisher specifically disclaim any responsibility for any liability, loss, or risk, personal or otherwise, which is incurred consequently, directly or indirectly, of the use and application of any of the contents of this book. Furthermore, the views and opinions expressed herein are solely those of the author and not influenced by any remuneration or financial gain from any third party.

Neither the author nor the publisher guarantees the accuracy of the information included in this book and are not responsible for any errors, omissions, or consequences from the application of the information presented. This book is for informational purposes only and does not constitute financial advice.

Acknowledgements

No matter how skilled a writer one may be, I recognise that my work is invariably enhanced by the input of friends and family. I'm deeply grateful to Martin, Huub, and Ze, who generously offered their time and insights to help me complete this project.

My heartfelt thanks go to my wonderful Wife and Children, who patiently read through my work and provided invaluable corrections. Your support means everything to me, and I love you all dearly.

Finally, I dedicate this to my beloved Mum, taken from us far too soon. Though you're no longer with us, your memory lives on in our hearts forever.

Contents

How to Use This Book

Introduction

Chapter 1 – Introduction to Padel Psychology	1
Chapter 2 – Building Confidence on the Court	21
Chapter 3 – Maintaining Focus During Matches	37
Chapter 4 – Managing Stress and Pressure	49
Chapter 5 – Developing a Winning Mindset	63
Chapter 6 – Visualisation Techniques for Padel Players	77
Chapter 7 – In-Game Mental Strategies	91
Chapter 8 – Overcoming Performance Anxiety	103
Chapter 9 – Dealing With Mistakes and Setbacks	113
Chapter 10 – Working With Your Partner	127

IMPORTANT: HOW TO USE THIS BOOK

Before you jump in and start reading cover to cover, I think it is important you know how this book is structured. There are many psychological aspects to consider in Padel, however this does not mean you are lacking the knowledge of how to deal with them. Maybe you struggle with maintaining focus or you get particularly anxious before or during a game. There are chapters in this book that address these issues.

I would therefore advise the following:

Start with Chapter 1 which will give you an insight into the importance of the mental game with Padel.

Have a look at the chapter titles and see which area you would like to work on first, and then jump to that chapter.

If you decide that you would like to read it chronologically, I suggest doing it slowly. The book asks you to practice many things, like you would do in your technical game, and to benefit the most from it, it is important to take your time and understand the process behind it.

INTRODUCTION

Thank you for picking up this book. Whether you're a beginner or an experienced player, if you're looking to elevate your padel game through psychological integration, you're in the right place. This book is your guide to achieving peak performance on the court.

Having spent over a decade guiding sports enthusiasts, I've encountered numerous misconceptions about padel. This experience, coupled with the prevalent questions I've received, inspired me to write this book. My goal is to help you improve your game by addressing both the physical and mental aspects of padel.

Many players find themselves struggling with unique challenges. Perhaps you've tried applying conventional tennis strategies to padel, only to find they fall short. Maybe you've struggled to find a consistent partner or coach who understands the mental demands of the game. Or you might feel stuck at a certain skill level, watching others advance while you plateau.

These frustrations often lead to what I call the "Cycle of False Starts." It begins with enthusiasm as you invest in new equipment or training. But progress stalls, leading to a plateau of discomfort. You seek shortcuts, experience temporary relief, only to realise you're back where you started. This cycle traps many players, leaving them anchored and unable to unlock their true potential.

What many fail to realise is that padel is as much a mental game as it is physical. While most players focus on perfecting their shots and strategies, the psychological aspect often receives little attention. This oversight can be the barrier between good and great performance.

Imagine stepping onto the court with unshakeable confidence, maintaining razor-sharp focus under pressure, and communicating seamlessly with your partner. Picture a mindset so resilient that setbacks become springboards for success. This isn't just a dream – it's achievable by integrating psychological strategies into your padel performance.

In this book, we'll explore key psychological aspects that

can transform your game. We'll work on building confidence, maintaining focus, managing stress and pressure, developing a winning mindset, utilising visualisation techniques, setting effective goals, overcoming performance anxiety, dealing with setbacks, and improving communication within the partnership.

Each chapter addresses these topics, providing practical tools and strategies to enhance your mental game. The book is structured to allow you to focus on the areas you need most. Feel free to skip to the chapters that address your specific challenges – there's no need to read it all in one sitting.

Are you ready to step out of the Cycle of False Starts and into a new era of padel excellence? Let's begin this journey together, transforming not just how you play, but how you think about the game. Let's begin this journey together.

CHAPTER 1

INTRODUCTION TO PADEL PSYCHOLOGY

'Resilience is not what happens to you. It's how you react to, respond to, and recover from what happens to you.' - Jeffrey Gitomer

The Importance of Mental Game in Padel

When stepping onto the padel court, what's really going through your mind? Is it just about how well you can swing your racket or how fast you can move? While physical skills are undeniably crucial, the mental game holds an equally, if not more significant, role in determining your success within those glass walls. Padel, like any sport, isn't just played on the court – it's also played in the mind.

Impact on Performance:

The mental game in padel is not just a supplementary aspect; it's a fundamental component that can make or break a player's performance. It influences every serve, every shot, and every decision you make during a match. High-pressure situations are common in padel, where a single point can often change the game's momentum. It's in these moments that mental strength becomes more than just an advantage – it becomes a necessity.

Consider the following ways in which psychology impacts padel:

- Shot Selection: A strong mental game allows players to make better tactical decisions under pressure. For instance, choosing between a defensive lob or an aggressive smash in a crucial point often comes down to mental clarity and confidence.

- Consistency: Mental focus helps maintain technique during long rallies. A lapse in concentration can lead to unforced errors, especially in the later stages of a match when fatigue sets in.

- Flexibility: The mental game enables players to quickly adjust to different opponents, playing styles, and court conditions. This flexibility is crucial in a sport where games can shift rapidly.

- Pressure Handling: In tie-breaks or match points, mental strength often determines the outcome more than technical skill.

Furthermore, your mental state affects your physical state. Stress and anxiety can tighten muscles, quicken breaths, and lead to mistakes and misjudgements. On the other hand, a positive, focused mental approach keeps you relaxed and sharp, with your energies channelled towards making precise and effective plays.

Differentiating Factor at Higher Levels:

As you climb higher in the ranks of padel players, the physical differences between competitors diminish. Everyone has great technique, everyone is fit, and everyone can hit winning shots. So, what separates the top players from the rest? More often than not, it's their mental game. While this applies to all levels of players, within the lower levels, there may be other differences such as, physical fitness that can determine who comes out on top.

At advanced levels, everyone practices hard, and everyone knows the game. But the best players are those who can consistently harness their mental power to face any challenge on the court. They are the ones who can keep their cool when the game heats up, who can turn a game around with sheer willpower, and who refuse to be intimidated by reputations or scoreboard pressure.

This mental edge becomes a crucial differentiator. It's about more than just being able to play well; it's about playing well when it counts. It involves managing emotions, maintaining focus, and executing strategies regardless of external pressures or immediate outcomes.

Specific examples at higher levels include:

- Marginal Gains: When physical and technical skills are closely matched, mental strength provides the edge. For example, the ability to stay focused during a long deuce game can be the difference between winning and losing a set.

- Consistency Across Tournaments: Mental toughness helps top players perform consistently across different tournaments and conditions. This is why some players are known for their ability to perform well in major events. Conversely, I have seen lower-level players, who perform well in social games, unable to reproduce the same form in a competition setting.

- Handling Media and Public Pressure: As padel grows in popularity, top players must deal with increased media scrutiny and public expectations. Mental resilience helps manage these external pressures.

- Balance Between Physical and Mental Skills: In padel, as in life, balance is key. While it's essential to have a high level of physical fitness, agility, and technical skills, these should be equally matched with strong mental skills. A well-rounded player who can leverage both aspects of the game often finds more success. Think of your mental skills as the hidden strategy behind every physical movement. For instance, strategic planning and anticipation require a sharp mind. Reading your opponent's intentions, predicting play patterns, and making split-second decisions are all cognitive processes that influence physical outcomes.

Achieving the right balance involves:

- Integrated Training: Incorporate mental training into physical drills. For example, practice serving under simulated pressure situations.

- Recovery and Preparation: Mental skills are vital for effective recovery within matches and preparation for upcoming games. Visualisation and relaxation techniques can be as important as physical warm-ups.

- Injury Management: A strong mental game aids in recovery from injuries, helping players stay positive and focused on rehabilitation.

Moreover, mental training can enhance your physical training. Visualisation techniques, for example, can improve your technique, timing, and accuracy, all without physically moving a muscle. By mentally rehearsing different play scenarios, you can condition your mind and body to perform optimally when it's game time.

Embracing the mental aspects of padel means you're not just working on your shots and stamina; you're also refining your mental tactics, emotional control, and stress management skills. This holistic approach can significantly elevate your game, giving you an edge that purely physical training cannot achieve.

Core Psychological Skills for Padel

Mastering the psychological aspects of padel can elevate your game, transforming good players into great ones. Let's look into the core psychological skills you can develop to boost your mental game in padel.

1. Self-awareness:

Understanding yourself is the cornerstone of any psychological skill set. In padel, this means being acutely aware of your own thoughts, emotions, and behaviours on the court. Self-awareness helps you recognise your typical reactions to stress, pressure, or disappointment during a match. It's about observing how you celebrate points, how you react to a missed shot, or how you handle a challenging opponent.

Developing self-awareness involves:

- Emotional Mapping: Identify how different emotions affect your play. For instance, does anger make you more aggressive but less accurate?

- Performance State Analysis: recognise your optimal arousal level. Some players perform best when calm, others when slightly excited.

- Trigger Identification: Pinpoint specific situations that affect your mental state, such as disputed line calls or crowd noise.

Techniques for improving self-awareness:

- Mindfulness Meditation: Practice 5-10 minutes daily, focusing on breath and bodily sensations.

- Match Reflection: After each match, spend 5 minutes thinking about your mental state during key moments.

- Video Analysis: Review match footage, paying attention to your body language and reactions.

- Journaling: Keep two padel diaries. The technical diary and the mental diary. In your technical diary, record 3 of your best shots. Do this each time you play so that after you have played a few times you can read about your best shots and store them in your memory bank. The majority of players will recall their mistakes more than their good shots. They will remember the shots that could have won the game but where they made an error. They completely forget the amazing shots that put them into the position to win the game in the first place.

2. Emotional Control:

Padel, like any competitive sport, can stir up a storm of emotions. From the thrill of a winning smash to the frustration of a faulty serve, how you manage these emotions can significantly impact your game. Emotional control is about maintaining balance, regardless of the court's highs and lows.

Emotional control in padel is crucial for maintaining performance:

- Anger Management: Learn to channel frustration into focused energy rather than letting it disrupt your play.

- Anxiety Control: Develop techniques to manage pre-match nerves and in-game tension.

- Positive Emotion Utilisation: Harness excitement and joy to enhance performance without losing focus.

Techniques for enhancing emotional control:

- Breath Control: Practice 4-7-8 breathing (in-hale for 4 counts, hold for 7, exhale for 8) during changeovers.

- Cognitive Reframing: Transform negative thoughts ("I always lose to this opponent") into positive ones ("Each match is a new opportunity").

- Anchoring: Develop a physical cue (e.g., touching the back glass) to trigger a calm state. (See Chapter 2)

- Visualisation: Before a match, visualise yourself playing calmly and confidently. Picture yourself handling tough points with composure.

- Short-term Goal Setting: Set short, manageable goals during the match to keep negative emotions at bay. Focus on winning the next point or playing a good shot rather than getting overwhelmed by the scoreline.

3. Mental Toughness:

The final piece of the psychological puzzle is mental toughness. This isn't just about pushing through when you're tired; it's about resilience, the ability to bounce back from setbacks, cognitive flexibility, and the determination to stick to your game plan under pressure. As Padel players, we often get sucked into the opponent's style of game when in fact, we need to stick to our own.

Mental toughness in padel encompasses:

- Resilience: The ability to bounce back from lost points, games, or matches.

- Focus: Maintaining concentration during long rallies and entire matches.

- Confidence: Belief in your abilities, especially when facing stronger opponents.

Developing mental toughness:

- Pressure Training: Regularly practice under simulated match conditions. Set up games where you start with a disadvantage to prepare for high-pressure situations.

- Adversity Scenarios: In training, create and overcome challenging situations (e.g., coming back from a 0-5 deficit).

- Goal Setting: Establish process goals (e.g., "stay aggressive on every point" " or keep calm") rather than just outcome goals.

- Focus on Controllables: Concentrate on elements you can control, such as your preparation, tactics, and response to each point, rather than worrying about external factors.

- Growth Mindset: Embrace a growth mindset, viewing each match, point, and shot as an opportunity to learn and improve. See failures as stepping stones to success or as opportunities for adjustments (cues to adjust).

4. Assessing Your Mental Game:

Take a step back and assess your mental game rigorously. This is done by evaluating where you stand mentally, you can identify what you need to work on to keep your head in the game just as much as your body. This is a crucial element of the psychological approach to the mental part of padel.

Self-evaluation Techniques:

Several methods can help you assess your mental game:

- Performance Journaling: Use your mental diary. After each match, rate (1-10) and describe your mental performance in areas like focus, emotional control, and confidence. Note what went through your mind at key moments, instances where you felt overwhelmed, anxious, or particularly confident.

- Video Analysis: Record your matches and review them, focusing on:

    • Body language during different scorelines
    • Reactions to errors and successful shots
    • Focus between points and during changeovers

- Psychometric Tests: Use sport-specific psychological assessments like the Athletic Coping Skills Inventory (ACSI) or the Psychological Performance Inventory (PPI) to measure mental skills like resilience, focus, and stress management.

- 360-Degree Feedback: Gather insights from coaches, playing partners, opponents, and even spectators about your on-court demeanour and mental approach.

5. Identifying Strengths and Weaknesses:

Once you have gathered initial data from your self-evaluation, the next step is to analyse this information to pinpoint your mental strengths and areas for improvement. Create a comprehensive mental skills profile, rating yourself from 1-10 in areas such as:

- Communication with doubles partner
- Concentration and focus
- Confidence and self-belief
- Emotional regulation
- Pressure handling
- Motivation and goal setting
- Resilience and ability to bounce back
- Pre-match preparation
- In-game strategy adaptation

Analyse patterns: Are your mental skills consistent across different match situations, or do they fluctuate? For instance, if your journal frequently notes feelings of nervousness during the first few points of a match, this might indicate that starting games strongly is a potential area for mental enhancement.

Conversely, you might find that you consistently note feeling in 'the zone' or at peak focus during long rallies.

This is a strength, and recognising it allows you to understand what conditions contribute to entering this optimal mental state.

It's also beneficial to seek feedback from others, such as coaches, teammates, or even opponents. They can offer valuable insights into your mental game that you might have missed.

6. Setting a Baseline for Improvement:

Having identified your mental strengths and weaknesses, it's time to set a baseline for your improvement. This baseline acts as a reference point from which you can measure progress towards your mental game goals.

Create a detailed mental game baseline:

1. Develop a Mental Skills Scorecard: Use your ratings to create a visual representation of your mental game profile.

2. Establish Key Performance Indicators (KPIs). For example:

- Percentage of points where focus was maintained
- Number of positive self-talk instances per set
- Recovery time after losing a game

3. Set SMART Goals: For each aspect of your mental game, set Specific, Measurable, Achievable, Relevant, and Time-bound goals. For instance, if your aim is to improve focus, your goal could be to maintain complete concentration for increasingly longer intervals during games.

4. Create an Improvement Plan: Based on your baseline, develop a structured plan to address weaknesses and enhance strengths.

5. Regular Reassessment: Schedule monthly or quarterly reviews of your mental game profile to track progress and adjust your improvement plan.

By thoroughly understanding and assessing these aspects of your mental game, you lay a solid foundation for targeted improvement. The goal here isn't just about becoming a better player—it's about becoming a more complete athlete, someone who harnesses the power of the mind to enhance physical performance.

RECAP AND ACTION ITEMS

By understanding the crucial role of mental acuity, you're already a step ahead in elevating your game. Remember, at higher levels, the physical differences between players narrow, and it's the mental edge that can set you apart. Balancing your mental and physical skills isn't just beneficial; it's essential.

Now, let's transform these insights into actionable steps to ensure you're not just absorbing information but applying it:

1. Self-Awareness Exercises: Start two padel journals. After each game or practice session, jot down what you felt in your mental journal, what went well, and what didn't. This reflection will enhance your self-awareness and help you notice patterns or recurring challenges. Do not forget to write down your three best shots in your technical journal. It will become more valuable as you continue to add to it.

2. Emotional Control Practices: Develop a routine that includes techniques such as deep breathing, meditation, or yoga to manage in-game stress. Try implementing these practices at least three times a week, and especially before matches, to cultivate a calmer, more composed presence on the court.

3. Boost Your Mental Toughness: Set small, achievable goals for each match or practice. Whether it's maintaining focus when down a point or managing frustration, these goals should challenge your mental resilience and encourage growth.

4. Self-Evaluation Routine: Every month, take time to review your journal and assess your emotional responses and mental toughness in various situations. Identify areas for improvement and adjust your training and mental strategies accordingly.

5. Strengths and Weaknesses Chart: Create a chart that lists your perceived strengths and weaknesses. Update this chart as you progress and use it to guide your practice focus areas.

6. Baseline Setting: Determine your current mental game baseline by asking a coach or a trusted teammate for their feedback on your psychological skills. Use this as a benchmark for measuring your improvement.

By taking these steps, you're not just playing padel; you're mastering it. The mental game is a vast and rich field, and you have the tools to cultivate resilience and sharpness that many players overlook. Keep these practices consistent, and watch as your game transforms, not just physically but mentally as well.

CHAPTER 2

BUILDING CONFIDENCE ON THE COURT

'Confidence comes not from always being right, but from not fearing to be wrong.' - Peter T. McIntyre

So, you have just stepped onto the court, what's the first thing that goes through your mind? Is it excitement, nervousness, anticipation or perhaps a mix of these? Whatever it is, one thing is certain: your level of confidence can have a significant effect on your performance. In padel, as in any sport, confidence isn't just a nice-to-have; it's a necessity. It's the foundation upon which great performances are built, the fuel that powers your shots, and the shield that protects you from doubt and fear.

1. Sources of Confidence in Padel

Confidence doesn't just appear out of thin air. It's built, nurtured, and reinforced through various sources. Let's explore the key pillars that support a padel player's confidence:

Past Successes:

Every point you've won, every match you've played, every challenge you've overcome - these are the building blocks of your confidence. But it's not just about remembering that you won; it's about understanding how you won and why. This is where keeping a detailed success (technical) journal becomes important.

Impact on Performance:

- Shot Selection: Remembering past successes can give you the courage to go for that winning shot when it matters most.

- Resilience: Recalling how you've bounced back before can help you stay positive when facing setbacks.

Think about expanding your success (technical) journal beyond just match outcomes. Include specific shots, strategies, or mental victories. For instance:

- "Executed a perfect lob over aggressive net players in third set."

- "Maintained composure after losing first set, came back to win match."

- "Successfully implemented new serving strategy throughout tournament."

Preparation and Training:

There's an old saying: "The more you sweat in training, the less you bleed in battle." This couldn't be truer for padel. Knowing that you've put in the hours, that you've practiced until your shots became second nature, that you've pushed your limits in training - this knowledge becomes a wellspring of confidence when you're on the court.

Impact on Performance:

- Consistency: Rigorous training leads to more consistent performance under pressure.

- Adaptability: Varied preparation allows you to confidently handle different playing styles and situations.

Develop a holistic training plan that includes the:

- Physical: Strength, agility, and endurance exercises specific to padel.

- Technical: Shot practice, footwork drills, wall practice for consistency.

- Tactical: Strategy sessions, video analysis of professional matches.

- Mental: Meditation, visualisation, pressure simulation drills, and positive self-dialogue.

Support from Partners and Coaches:

Padel is unique in its emphasis on partnership. The support and belief of your doubles partner can be a powerful confidence booster. We will discuss this in more detail in Chapter 10 - Working with Your Partner. Similarly, the guidance and feedback from a trusted coach can help you see improvements you might have missed and areas where you excel.

Impact on Performance:

- Communication: Strong support systems improve on-court communication and decision-making.
- Motivation: Positive reinforcement from partners and coaches can fuel your drive to improve.

Cultivate a "performance team":

- Regular check-ins with your coach to discuss progress and challenges
- Develop a pre-match routine with your doubles partner
- Consider working with a sports psychologist for personalised mental strategies
- Join or create a padel support group to share experiences and tips

2. Techniques to Boost Self-Confidence

Now that we understand where confidence comes from, let's look at practical techniques to boost it:

Positive Self-Talk:

The voice in your head can be your biggest cheerleader or your worst critic. Learning to harness the power of positive self-talk can transform your mental game. It is important to already believe in what you are saying to yourself, and, in this case, you are just reminding yourself of this rather than listening to the often-automatic negative talk. If you do not, then it is important to go back and work on building your self-confidence.

Impact on Performance:

- Resilience: Positive self-talk can help you bounce back from mistakes more quickly.

- Focus: It can keep you centered on the task at hand rather than dwelling on errors.

Use your mental journal and create a personalised "self-talk playbook" within it:

- List common challenging situations in padel (e.g. facing match point, playing a stronger opponent).

- Develop 2-3 positive phrases for each situation e.g. I have done this before.
- Practice these phrases regularly, even outside of matches.

Body Language and Posture:

Your body language doesn't just communicate to others; it communicates to yourself. Standing tall, moving purposefully, and maintaining an open posture can actually make you feel more confident.

Impact on Performance:

- Intimidation Factor: Confident body language can intimidate opponents, without necessarily looking aggressive.
- Energy Levels: Positive posture can increase energy and reduce fatigue.

Implement the "Confidence Stance":

- Stand tall with shoulders back and chest open
- Make eye contact with your partner and opponents
- Use deliberate, purposeful movements between points

- Practice "power poses" during breaks

Confidence Routines:

Developing a consistent pre-match routine can help you get into the right mental state before stepping onto the court.

Impact on Performance:

- Consistency: Routines provide a sense of familiarity and control, leading to more consistent performances.
- Focus: They help you transition into a competitive mindset.

Develop a comprehensive pre-match routine:

1. Physical warm-up (15-20 minutes)
2. Technical warm-up with partner (10-15 minutes)
3. Mental preparation (5-10 minutes):
    - Listen to 2-3 pump-up songs
    - Visualise successful play for 2-3 minutes
    - Repeat personal mantra 3 times
4. Final equipment check and hydration

3. Overcoming Self-Doubt

Even the most confident players experience self-doubt. The key is not to eliminate it entirely (which is unrealistic), but to manage it effectively:

Identifying Negative Thought Patterns:

The first step in overcoming self-doubt is recognising when it's happening. Often, negative thoughts follow predictable patterns.

Impact on Performance:

- Self-Awareness: recognising thought patterns allows for quicker intervention.

- Emotional Control: Understanding your triggers helps manage emotional responses.

Reframing Negative Thoughts:

Once you've identified negative thoughts, the next step is to challenge and reframe them.

Practice the "ABCDE" method:

- **A**dversity: Identify the challenging situation

- **B**eliefs: Notice your automatic thoughts about the situation

- **C**onsequences: recognise how these beliefs affect your emotions and behaviour

- **D**ispute: Challenge these beliefs with evidence and logic by asking yourself 3 questions (is this thought completely true, helpful, or kind to myself?)

- **E**nergization: Create a new, empowering belief and action plan

Try the Diffusion technique:

Our mind tends to fuse with our negative thoughts, making us believe them, especially the negative ones, leading us to operate through several cognitive biases. From an evolutionary point of view, this makes sense, as it has the function of protecting us from danger or unpleasant events. However, the flip side to this is that NAT (negative automatic thoughts) trigger secondary negative emotions such as anxiety or anger, leading to physiological responses and a change in behaviour as we fuse (believe them). We can start learning how to diffuse from them by:

- Identifying what is going on
- Practicing seeing thoughts as thoughts rather than 100 percent reality
- Then refocusing our attention on what is in front of us

Impact on Performance:

- Resilience: Reframing helps you bounce back from setbacks more quickly.
- Problem-Solving: It encourages a more constructive approach to challenges.

Building Resilience:

Resilience is the ability to bounce back from setbacks. It's a crucial skill in padel, where momentum can shift rapidly.

Impact on Performance:

- Consistency: Resilient players maintain performance levels even after setbacks.

- Long-term Improvement: A resilient mindset facilitates learning and growth.

Implement a "Growth Mindset" approach:

- View challenges as opportunities for learning and improvement

- Celebrate effort and progress, not just outcomes

- After each match, identify 3 areas for improvement

- Develop a "bounce-back" routine for handling setbacks

RECAP AND ACTION ITEMS

1. Positive Self-Talk

- Understand the power of positive self-talk in boosting confidence

2. Body Language and Posture

- Recognise how your body language affects your confidence and opponents' perception

- Implement the "Confidence Stance":

    - Stand tall with shoulders back and chest open
    - Make eye contact with your partner and opponents
    - Use deliberate, purposeful movements between points
    - Practice "power poses" during breaks

3. Confidence Routines

- Develop a consistent pre-match routine to enhance mental preparation

- Create your comprehensive pre-match routine:

    - Physical warm-up (15-20 minutes)
    - Technical warm-up with partner (10-15 minutes)
    - Mental preparation (5-10 minutes): music, visualisation, personal mantra
    - Final equipment check and hydration

4. Identifying and Reframing Negative Thoughts

- Learn to recognise negative thought patterns and their impact

- Practice the "ABCDE" method:

    - **A**dversity: Identify the challenging situation
    - **B**eliefs: Notice your automatic thoughts
    - **C**onsequences: Recognise how these beliefs affect you
    - **D**ispute: Challenge these beliefs with evidence and logic
    - **E**nergization: Create a new, empowering belief and action plan

5. Building Resilience

- Understand the importance of bouncing back from setbacks in padel

- Implement a "Growth Mindset" approach:

    - View challenges as opportunities for learning and improvement

- Celebrate effort and progress, not just outcomes
- After each match, identify 3 areas for improvement
- Develop a "bounce-back" routine for handling setbacks

6. Continuous Improvement

- Remember that building confidence is an ongoing process

- Consistently practice these mental techniques alongside your physical padel skills

- Regularly review and refine your mental game strategies

By implementing these strategies and continuously working on your mental game, you'll develop a robust sense of self-belief that will enhance your performance both on and off the padel court.

In the next chapter, we'll explore how to maintain focus and concentration during high-pressure situations in padel matches.

CHAPTER 3

MAINTAINING FOCUS DURING MATCHES

'The successful warrior is the average man, with laser-like focus.' - Bruce Lee

When the serve is made, the rally begins, and the intensity builds, where does your mind wander? Are you fully present in the moment, or do you find your thoughts drifting to the scoreboard, your last error, or even what you'll have for dinner? In padel, as in life, our ability to focus can make the difference between victory and defeat. But what exactly is focus in the context of our sport, and how can we harness its power to elevate our game?

1. Understanding Focus in Padel

Focus isn't just about concentrating hard; it's about concentrating on the right things at the right time. In the fast-paced world of padel, where split-second decisions can turn the tide of a match, understanding and mastering different types of attention is crucial.

Types of Attention:

In padel, players need to juggle various forms of attention:

- Selective Attention: Filtering out irrelevant stimuli and focusing on what truly matters at that moment, like keeping your eye on the ball, regardless of the movement around you. This sounds obvious however many players forget and move their eyes to their opponents or something else that catches their eye.

- Divided Attention: The multitasking aspect of focus. Simultaneously keeping track of the ball, your position, your partner's position, and your opponents' positions and strategies.

- Sustained Attention: Maintaining a consistent level of concentration over an extended period, crucial for those long, gruelling matches.

Impact on Performance:

- Shot Selection: Proper focus allows for better reading of the game and smarter shot choices.
- Reaction Time: Maintaining the right type of attention can improve your ability to respond quickly to an opponent's shots.
- Consistency: Sustained focus leads to fewer unforced errors and more consistent play.

Common Distractions in Padel:

Padel courts are rife with potential distractions. Some are external, like crowd noise, other people chatting on the side of your court or weather conditions. Others are internal, such as self-doubt or fatigue. Understanding these distractions is the first step in learning to manage them:

- External Distractions: Noise from adjacent courts, weather conditions, spectator comments, opponents' reactions

- Internal Distractions: Negative self-talk, anxiety about the score, physical discomfort, negative predictions, anger and frustration

- Tactical Distractions: Overthinking strategy, focusing too much on opponent's strengths

The Cost of Lost Focus:

Losing focus during a padel match isn't just about missing a few points. It can have cascading effects on your overall gameplay and mental state:

- Missed Opportunities: A lack of focus can mean failing to capitalise on an opponent's weak shot.

- Unforced Errors: Distraction often leads to simple mistakes that could have been avoided.

- Tactical Missteps: Poor focus can result in forgetting game plans or failing to adapt to changing match conditions.

- Momentum Shifts: A sudden lapse in concentration can let your opponent back into the game, reversing momentum.

2. Concentration Techniques

Now that we understand the importance of focus, how do we cultivate and maintain it during a match?

Pre-point Routines:

Developing a consistent routine before each point can help center your mind and prepare your body for action.

Impact on Performance:

- Consistency: Routines provide a sense of control and familiarity, leading to more consistent play.

- Transition: They help you shift focus from the previous point to the present moment.

Consider implementing a routine that includes:

- Physical reset: Adjust grip, bounce on toes

- Deep breath: Oxygenate your body and calm your mind

- Visualisation: Briefly picture your intended serve or return

- Cue word: Use a personal trigger word to snap into focus (e.g., "Ready" or "Now")

Breathing Exercises:

Controlled breathing is a powerful tool for maintaining focus and managing arousal levels.

Try the 4-7-8 technique:

- Inhale slowly through your nose for four seconds
- Hold your breath for seven seconds
- Exhale completely through your mouth for eight seconds

For an in-game focus boost, use tactical breathing:

- Inhale and exhale in short, controlled bursts to maintain an optimal arousal state

Anchoring Techniques:

Anchoring involves associating a specific physical action with a desired mental state. For example, imagine you have just made what you consider to be the most ridiculous error and now you must serve again. Before you serve, find something that triggers you to regain your focus.

Develop your anchor:

- Choose a discrete physical action (e.g., touching a point on your bat, adjusting your wristband)
- Practice performing this action while in a highly focused state during training
- Use the anchor during matches to quickly trigger a focused mindset

3. Regaining Focus When Distracted

Even with the best techniques, distractions will occur. The key is how quickly and effectively you can refocus.

Quick Reset Strategies:

Having a go-to method for regaining focus can save crucial points.

Try these reset strategies:

- The "3-Second Rule": Allow yourself three seconds to acknowledge a distraction, then deliberately refocus
- Physical Reset: Use a brief physical routine (e.g., adjusting your cap, retying shoelaces) as a cue to refocus
- Mental Imagery: Quickly visualise your "ideal performance state" to reset your focus

Refocusing Cues:

Verbal or visual cues can serve as powerful tools to redirect attention.

Develop personal refocusing cues:

- Choose a word or phrase that resonates with you (e.g., "Present," "Next point")
- Select a visual cue on your racket or clothing to draw your eyes to
- Practice using these cues in training to build the habit

Adapting to Environmental Factors:

Different playing conditions require different focusing strategies.

Strategies for adapting:

- Simulate various conditions in practice (e.g., noise, wind) to develop coping strategies

- Develop a pre-match routine to assess and mentally prepare for the specific court conditions

- Use visualisation techniques to imagine performing well in challenging environments

RECAP AND ACTION ITEMS

This chapter has equipped you with an arsenal of techniques and strategies to help you maintain and regain your focus, ensuring you're performing at your best every time you step onto the court.

Let's action what you've learned:

1. **Implement Pre-Point Routines:** Develop a consistent set of actions before each point.

2. **Practice Breathing Exercises:** Integrate techniques like the 4-7-8 method into your training and pre-match routines.

3. **Explore Anchoring Techniques:** Create a physical or mental anchor to bring your focus back when needed.

4. **Use Quick Reset Strategies:** Prepare strategies to quickly regain focus after distractions.

5. **Develop Refocusing Cues:** Create personal cues that can swiftly bring back your concentration.

6. **Adapt to Environmental Factors:** Plan strategies to cope with various environ- mental conditions.

Remember, focus is a skill that can be developed and refined, much like your backhand or serve. Regular practice of these techniques will make them second nature, allowing you to stay calm and focused even in high-pressure situations. By integrating these tools into your routine, you're not just improving your game technically but also mentally. Keep practicing, stay mindful, and watch as your game transforms on the padel court.

CHAPTER 4

MANAGING STRESS AND PRESSURE

'Pressure is a privilege -- it only comes to those who earn it.' - Billie Jean King

How do you respond when things get tight and heated on the court? Do you rise to the occasion or let expectations pull you down? In the physically and cognitively demanding sport of padel, your ability to handle stress and pressure makes all the difference between not only winning and losing but also between the enjoyment you get from the whole experience. This chapter will arm you with powerful strategies to not only withstand the heat of competition but to harness that energy and turn pressure into your secret weapon.

1. The Nature of Stress and Pressure in Padel

Stress and pressure are inherent parts of competitive padel. They can manifest in various ways:

- Physical: Increased heart rate, sweaty palms, muscle tension

- Mental: Racing thoughts, difficulty concentrating, self-doubt

- Emotional: Anxiety, irritability, mood swings

Impact on Performance:

- Shot Selection: Pressure can lead to conservative play or reckless decisions

- Technique: Stress often causes players to revert to old habits or lose form

- Tactics: Lack of focus can impair strategic thinking and adaptability

Consider how stress affects different aspects of your game:

- Serve: Does your first serve percentage drop in crucial moments?

- Volleys: Do you find yourself less aggressive at the net when the stakes are high?

- Movement: Does pressure make you feel sluggish or overly tense on court?

Understanding your personal stress response is the first step in managing it effectively.

2. Recognising Stress Symptoms

Developing awareness of your stress symptoms is crucial. Here's what to look out for:

Physical Signs:

- Muscle tension, especially in shoulders and grip

- Rapid breathing

- Stomach discomfort or nausea

- Fatigue or sudden energy spikes

Emotional Indicators:

- Irritability or frustration with partner or opponents
- Anxiety or excessive worry about the outcome
- Loss of confidence or negative self-talk
- Difficulty enjoying the game

Behavioural Changes:

- Changes in communication with your partner
- Alterations in pre-match routines or superstitions
- Procrastination in practice or match preparation
- Seeking excessive reassurance from coach or supporters

Impact on Performance:

- Inconsistent play due to physical tension
- Poor decision-making from emotional instability
- Decreased shot accuracy and power
- Impaired coordination and timing

3. Stress Management Techniques

Now that we understand how stress manifests, let's look at some effective techniques to manage it:

Progressive Muscle Relaxation (PMR):

This technique involves systematically tensing and relaxing different muscle groups. It's particularly effective for releasing physical tension that can accumulate during intense matches.

How to practice PMR:

1. Find a comfortable position

2. Starting from your feet, tense each muscle group for 5-10 seconds

3. Release the tension abruptly and feel the relaxation

4. Move upwards through your body to your face

5. Practice regularly, especially after training sessions or matches

Impact on Performance:

- Reduced muscle tension, leading to improved flexibility and reaction time.

- Enhanced body awareness, allowing for better shot control.

- Quicker recovery between points and games.

Mindfulness and Meditation:

These practices help center your thoughts and emotions, crucial for maintaining focus during fast-paced padel matches.

Implementing mindfulness:

1. Start with short, 5-minute daily meditation sessions

2. Focus on your breath, observing thoughts without judgement

3. Gradually increase duration and apply mindfulness to training

4. During practice, focus entirely on each movement and sensation

Impact on Performance:

- Improved focus and concentration during crucial points.

- Better emotional regulation in high-pressure situations.
- Enhanced ability to stay present and adapt to changing game conditions.

Cognitive Restructuring:

This technique involves identifying and challenging negative thoughts, replacing them with more positive, realistic ones.

Practicing cognitive restructuring:

1. Use your mental journal after games

2. Identify negative thoughts (e.g., "I always mess up under pressure")

3. Challenge these thoughts with evidence

4. Reframe them positively (e.g., "I've handled pressure well before and can do it again")

Impact on Performance:

- Increased confidence in high-stakes situations.
- Reduced performance anxiety.

- Improved resilience after setbacks.

4. Performing Under Pressure

Embracing pressure situations is key to excelling in padel. Here's how to make pressure your ally:

Reframing Pressure:

Instead of viewing pressure as a threat, see it as a challenge and an opportunity to showcase your skills. This shift in perspective can transform your performance.

Techniques for reframing:

- Positive self-talk: "This is my chance to shine" instead of "I hope I don't mess up"

- Focusing on process goals rather than outcomes

- Embracing the physical symptoms of pressure as signs of readiness

Pressure Simulation in Practice:

Create conditions in training that mimic high-pressure match situations. This prepares you mentally and physically for real competitive scenarios.

Ideas for pressure simulation:

- Set up match-point scenarios in practice
- Introduce consequences for losing points (e.g., extra conditioning such as push ups)
- Practice with an audience or under video recording

Developing a Pressure-Proof Routine:

Establish a series of actions to perform before each game or point. This provides a sense of control and familiarity in high-stress moments.

Elements of a pre-point routine:

- Deep breath to center yourself
- Visualisation of successful execution

- Physical reset (e.g., racket grip adjustment)
- Positive affirmation or cue word

Impact on Performance:

- Increased comfort in high-stakes situations.
- Improved decision-making under pressure.
- Enhanced ability to maintain technique and strategy when it matters most.
- Greater enjoyment of competitive challenges.

RECAP AND ACTION ITEMS

You've now explored the intricacies of recognising stress symptoms, various stress management techniques, and strategies for performing under pressure. Each of these elements is crucial not only for your success on the padel court but for your overall well-being as an athlete.

1. Use your mental journal: Note any physical, emotional, or behavioural signs of stress you experience in and out of sport. Review weekly to identify patterns.

Try and work on these one by one until you feel you can cross an item off the journal.

2. Daily relaxation practice: Dedicate at least 10 minutes daily to either progressive muscle relaxation or meditation. Use an app or timer to stay consistent.

3. Thought reframing: Introduce cognitive restructuring into your weekly routine. Identify at least one negative thought each week and actively reframe it. Write down both the original thought and its positive counterpart.

4. Pressure simulation: Plan a monthly pressure simulation session. Work with your coach or partner to create scenarios where you must perform under heightened stress. Gradually increase the intensity of these simulations.

5. Develop your pre-match routine: Create a comprehensive pre-match routine that incorporates elements of muscle relaxation, mindfulness, and mental preparation. Practice this routine before every match, refining it as needed.

6. Positive pressure reminders: Place reminders (e.g., wristband, racket sticker) with positive pressure-related mantras. Use these as quick reframing tools during matches.

7. Post-match reflection: After each match, spend 10 minutes reflecting on how you handled pressure. Note what worked well and areas for improvement.

Remember, managing stress and pressure isn't just about better performance on the court—it's about enhancing your overall quality of life. Every step you take builds resilience, not just as a player, but as a person. Embrace these practices, and watch as your mental game transforms, allowing you to perform at your best when it matters most.

In our next chapter, we'll build on these stress management techniques as we explore the crucial topic of 'Developing a Winning Mindset'. We'll see how to cultivate a positive, resilient attitude that can turn challenges into opportunities and setbacks into comebacks. The mental toughness you're developing now will serve as the foundation for this winning mindset, and more enjoyment of the padel game.

Stay committed to your mental training and see how you start thriving on the padel court.

CHAPTER 5

DEVELOPING A WINNING MINDSET

'It is not the strongest of the species that survive, nor the most intelligent, but the one most responsive to change.'
- Charles Darwin

As you progress in your padel journey, you'll discover that the difference between good players and great ones often lies not in their physical abilities, but in their mental approach to the game. A winning mindset is the secret weapon that can elevate your performance, turning challenges into opportunities and setbacks into comebacks.

In this chapter, we'll look at the psychological toolkit of champion padel players. We'll explore how to cultivate a growth mindset that thrives on challenges, builds resilience that bounces back from adversity, and develops the mental toughness that allows you to perform at your best when the pressure is on.

Whether you're at a beginner level looking to build a strong mental foundation or an experienced player aiming to refine your psychological game, the strategies and techniques we'll discuss can transform your approach to padel. By the end of this chapter, you'll have a comprehensive understanding of what it takes to think like a champion, and more importantly, how to put these principles into practice both on and off the court.

1. Characteristics of a Champion's Mindset

Impact on Performance:

A champion's mindset influences every serve, every shot, and every decision you make during a match. It's the foundation upon which great performances are built, the fuel that powers your shots, and the shield that protects you from doubt and fear.

Consider the following ways in which a champion's mindset impacts padel performance:

- Decision Making: A strong mindset allows players to make better tactical decisions under pressure. For instance, choosing between a defensive lob or an aggressive smash in a crucial point often comes down to mental clarity and confidence.

- Consistency: Mental focus helps maintain technique during long rallies. A lapse in concentration can lead to unforced errors, especially in the later stages of a match when fatigue sets in.

- Adaptability: The champion's mindset enables players to quickly adjust to different opponents, playing styles, and court conditions. This flexibility is crucial in a sport where games can shift rapidly.

- Pressure Handling: In tie-breaks or match points, mental strength often determines the outcome more than technical skill.

Let's focus on the core aspects that make up this mindset:

Growth vs. Fixed Mindset:

A growth mindset, coined by psychologist Carol Dweck, is the belief that abilities and intelligence can be developed through dedication and hard work. In contrast, a fixed mindset assumes that our character, intelligence, and creative ability are static givens which we can't change in any meaningful way.

Developing a Growth Mindset:

- Embrace challenges: Seek out tough opponents and new playing styles.

- Learn from criticism: View feedback as constructive, not personal.

- Find lessons in others' success: Instead of feeling threatened by opponents' skills, get inspired to improve your own.

Resilience and Adaptability:

Resilience is the ability to recover from difficulties, while adaptability is about adjusting to new conditions. In the dynamic world of padel, both are crucial.

Building Resilience and Adaptability:

- Practice adversity: Intentionally put yourself in challenging situations during training.

- Reflect on setbacks: After each loss, identify what you learned and how you can improve.

- Develop a broad skill set: Practice various playing styles to increase your adaptability. While this in itself is not a mental skill, it will give you confidence to challenge all types of opponents.

Passion and Commitment:

True champions are driven by a deep love for the game and an unwavering commitment to improvement.

Nurturing Passion and Commitment:

- Set meaningful goals: Align your padel objectives with your personal values.

- Celebrate small wins: Acknowledge progress to fuel your motivation.

- Connect with the padel community: Engage with other passionate players to keep your enthusiasm high.

2. Cultivating a Positive Attitude

A positive attitude isn't just about feeling good – it's a powerful tool for performance enhancement in padel. Here are some key techniques to foster positivity:

Gratitude Practices:

Regularly acknowledging the good in your padel journey, can shift your entire perspective.

Implementing Gratitude:

- Using your technical journal: Monthly, write three things you're grateful for in your padel experience.

- Express appreciation: Thank your partners, coaches, and even opponents for the role they play in your development.

- Gratitude warm-up: Before each match, mentally list three things you're grateful for about the opportunity to play.

Impact on Performance:

- Reduced Stress: Gratitude practices lower cortisol levels, improving physical performance.

- Enhanced Teamwork: Appreciative players often have better relationships with partners and coaches.

- Increased Enjoyment: Finding joy in the process leads to more consistent effort and improvement.

Optimism Training:

Optimism in padel isn't about ignoring challenges, but about believing in your ability to overcome them.

Cultivating Optimism:

- Positive self-talk: Replace negative self-talk with encouraging, realistic statements.

- Visualise success: Regularly imagine yourself performing well and achieving your goals.

- Learn optimistic explanatory style: Attribute successes to your skills and effort and see setbacks as temporary and specific.

Impact on Performance:

- Confidence: Optimistic players tend to have higher self-confidence.

- Persistence: Optimism fuels the determination to keep trying in the face of challenges.

- Problem-Solving: Optimistic players are more likely to seek solutions rather than dwell on problems.

Reframing Challenges as Opportunities:

The ability to see difficulties as chances for growth is a hallmark of champions.

Reframing Techniques:

- Ask empowering questions: Instead of "Why is this happening to me?", ask "What can I learn from this?"

- Find the benefit: For every challenge, identify at least one potential positive outcome.

- Create a challenge mindset: View each match as an opportunity to test and improve your skills.

Impact on Performance:

- Reduced Anxiety: Seeing challenges positively lowers performance anxiety as whatever happens is an information to work with rather than a threat.

- Increased Engagement: Players who view challenges as opportunities tend to be more engaged in training and matches.

- Improved Learning: A positive approach to challenges accelerates skill development.

3. Mental Toughness in Padel

Mental toughness is often the deciding factor in close matches and high-pressure situations. Let's explore its components and how to develop it:

Defining Mental Toughness:

Mental toughness in padel is the ability to consistently perform towards the upper range of your skill level, regardless of competitive circumstances.

Components of Mental Toughness:

- Focus: The ability to concentrate on relevant cues and ignore distractions.

- Confidence: Belief in your abilities, even under pressure.

- Control: Managing your emotions and reactions effectively.

- Commitment: Dedication to your goals, even when faced with obstacles.

- (Refer to Chapter 1 for more detail.)

Building Mental Stamina:

Just like physical stamina, mental stamina can be developed through consistent training.

Mental Stamina Exercises:

- Mindfulness meditation: Regular meditation enhances your ability to stay present and focused.

- Pressure simulation: Create high-pressure scenarios in practice to build mental endurance.

Impact on Performance:

- Consistency: Mentally tough players perform more consistently across different conditions.

- Clutch Performance: The ability to execute skills effectively in high-pressure situations.

- Resilience: Quicker recovery from setbacks and maintaining confidence in challenging times.

Overcoming Adversity:

Champions are defined not by their lack of adversity, but by how they respond to it.

Adversity Management Strategies:

- Develop a growth narrative: Frame setbacks as part of your growth journey, not as failures.

- Create an adversity response plan: Have a set of steps to follow when facing difficulties.

- Practice self-compassion: Treat yourself with kindness and understanding in tough times (ask yourself how you would respond towards a person who you respect).

Impact on Performance:

- Faster Recovery: Players who manage adversity well bounce back quicker from losses.

- Learning Orientation: Adversity is viewed as a chance to learn and improve.

- Emotional Stability: Less performance fluctuation due to external circumstances.

RECAP AND ACTION ITEMS

This chapter has looked at some crucial elements of developing a winning mindset in padel. From cultivating a growth mindset to building mental toughness, you're now better equipped with the tools to elevate your mental game.

Here are your action steps to integrate these lessons into your padel practice:

1. Mindset Check-in: At the end of each week, reflect on your mindset. Were you growth-oriented or fixed? Write down specific examples.

2. Optimism Challenge: For the next month, consciously reframe one negative thought into a positive one each day.

3. Resilience Building: After each match or challenging practice, think about what you learned and how you can apply it to future improvement.

4. Mental Toughness Training: Incorporate one mental toughness exercise (e.g., concentration/focus, mindfulness meditation) into your daily routine.

5. Adversity Response Plan: Create a personal step-by-step plan for dealing with setbacks. Practice following this plan in your next challenging situation.

6. Positive Self-Talk: Develop three personal mantras that embody your ideal mindset. Repeat these during training and matches.

Remember, developing a winning mindset is an ongoing process. It is a state of mind that you must learn to believe, and it requires consistent effort and practice, just like any physical skill in padel. Embrace this journey of mental growth, and you'll find that it not only elevates your game but enriches your entire padel experience.

In our next chapter, we'll explore the powerful technique of visualisation and how it can enhance your performance on the padel court. We still have much to learn about how to harness the power of your mind to improve your physical game.

CHAPTER 6

VISUALISATION TECHNIQUES FOR PADEL PLAYERS

'Imagination is everything. It is the preview of life's coming attractions.' - Albert Einstein

1. Fundamentals of visualisation

Visualisation, the art of creating vivid mental experiences, is a powerful tool that can significantly enhance your performance in padel. It's not just about seeing; it's about fully experiencing the game in your mind before you step onto the court. This technique harnesses the power of your mind to influence your physical behaviour and can be a significant factor in how you prepare and perform.

Creating Vivid Mental Images:

To master visualisation, start by creating detailed mental images of your padel experiences. Close your eyes and imagine your favourite court, focusing on specific details like the texture of the surface, the surrounding nets, and the lighting conditions.

Impact on Performance:

- Enhanced muscle memory through mental rehearsal.
- Improved focus and concentration during actual play.

Techniques for vivid imagery:

- Start with familiar scenes and gradually add more complex elements
- Practice regularly to improve the clarity and detail of your mental images

Incorporating All Senses:

Effective visualisation engages all your senses, creating a more immersive and realistic mental experience.

Impact on Performance:

- More lifelike mental rehearsals, better preparing you for actual play.

- Stronger emotional engagement, boosting confidence and reducing anxiety.

Multi-sensory visualisation techniques:

- Focus on tactile sensations like the grip of your racket and the feel of the court surface

- Incorporate sounds such as the ball hitting the wall and your partner's calls

- Include olfactory elements like the fresh outdoor air or the unique scent of an indoor arena

Timing and Frequency of Practice:

Consistent, well-timed visualisation practice is key to reaping its benefits.

Impact on Performance:

- Accelerated skill acquisition through regular mental practice.

- Enhanced pre-competition preparation and focus.

Guidelines for visualisation practice:

- Aim for daily sessions of 5-10 minutes, particularly during calm periods like early morning or before bed

- Incorporate visualisation into your pre-match routine for optimal performance preparation

2. Types of Visualisations for Padel

Different visualisation techniques can be employed to enhance various aspects of your padel game:

Outcome Visualisation:

This involves imagining successful end results, such as winning a match or achieving a specific ranking.

Impact on Performance:

- Increased motivation and commitment to training.

- Enhanced confidence and reduced performance anxiety.

Implementing outcome visualisation:

- Set realistic, achievable goals for your visualisations
- Engage all senses to make the imagined success feel more tangible
- Balance outcome visualisation with process-focused imagery

Process Visualisation:

This type focuses on the step-by-step execution of skills or strategies.

Impact on Performance:

- Improved technique through mental rehearsal of correct form.
- Enhanced decision-making skills in match situations.

Techniques for process visualisation:

- Break down complex shots and visualise each component separately
- Use slow-motion imagery to focus on precise details

- Practice from a first-person perspective for a more immersive experience

Performance Rehearsal:

This involves mentally simulating entire match scenarios, including potential challenges and your responses.

Impact on Performance:

- Improved adaptability to various game situations.

- Reduced anxiety through mental preparation for different scenarios.

Implementing performance rehearsal:

- Create realistic match scenarios in your mind, including opponent strategies

- Practice problem-solving and emotional control in your visualisations

- Incorporate performance rehearsal into your pre-match preparation

3. Applying Visualisation in Padel

Pre-match Imagery:

Using visualisation as part of your pre-match routine can help prime your mind and body for optimal performance.

Impact on Performance:

- Improved focus and reduced pre-match anxiety.
- Enhanced confidence and mental readiness.

Implementing pre-match visualisation:

- Find a quiet spot to center your thoughts before the match
- Visualise yourself entering the court confidently and playing well
- Engage all senses to make the mental rehearsal as realistic as possible

Shot-specific Visualisation:

Mentally rehearsing individual shots can enhance technique and consistency.

Impact on Performance:

- Refined technique through repeated mental practice.
- Increased confidence in specific shots or strategies.

Techniques for shot-specific visualisation:

- Focus on one shot at a time, visualising perfect execution
- Practice off-court, using spare moments throughout your day
- Combine mental rehearsal with physical practice for maximum benefit

Visualising Successful Problem-solving:

Mental rehearsal of overcoming challenges can improve your adaptability and resilience on court.

Impact on Performance:

- Enhanced tactical flexibility and decision-making under pressure.

- Improved mental toughness and ability to handle adversity.

Implementing problem-solving visualisation:

- Imagine common challenges you face in matches

- Visualise yourself adapting and overcoming these obstacles

- Practice communicating effectively with your partner in challenging situations

RECAP AND ACTION ITEMS

We have introduced just some ideas of the powerful world of visualisation techniques for padel. You've learned about creating vivid mental images, incorporating all senses, and applying various types of visualisations to enhance your game. Now it's time to put these techniques into practice.

Here are your action steps to integrate visualisation into your padel training and match preparation:

1. **Daily Visualisation Practice:**

   - Set aside 5-10 minutes each day for visualisation exercises.

   - Start with a simple scene, like serving an ace, and gradually build up to more complex scenarios.

   - Use a timer or meditation app to maintain consistency.

2. **Multi-Sensory Visualisation:**

   - Keep track of your visualisation practice. If necessary, use your mental journal to remind yourself of the occasions when you have been able to use this technique with success.

   - After each session, think about what you saw, felt, heard, smelled, and even tasted in your mental imagery.

   - Practice increasing the vividness of each sense over time.

3. Pre-Match Visualisation Routine:

- Develop a 5-minute pre-match visualisation routine.

- Include elements like confidently entering the court, successfully executing key shots, and effectively communicating with your partner.

- Practice this routine before every match for at least a month to establish it as a habit.

4. Shot-Specific Mental Practice:

- Choose one shot you want to improve each week.

- Spend 3-5 minutes daily visualising the perfect execution of this shot.

- Combine this mental practice with physical repetitions during your training sessions.

5. Problem-Solving Scenarios:

- Create a list of 5-10 common challenges you face in matches (e.g., aggressive net players, tricky serves).

- Dedicate one visualisation session per week to mentally rehearsing overcoming these challenges.

- After each real match, add any new challenges you encountered to your list.

6. Outcome and Process Balance:

- Alternate between outcome and process visualisation in your practice.

- On even days, focus on visualising successful outcomes (winning matches, achieving rankings).

- On odd days, concentrate on the process (perfect technique, strategic decision-making).

7. Visualisation Performance Log:

- After each match, think about how well your actual performance aligned with your visualisations. To be more efficient, try writing some of these in your mental journal.

- Note any discrepancies and use these insights to refine your future visualisation practice.

8. Partner Visualisation Sessions:

- If possible, schedule weekly visualisation sessions with your doubles partner.
- Focus on teamwork scenarios, effective communication, and complementary strategies.

9. Sensory Enhancement Exercises:

- Spend time on the court with your eyes closed, focusing on the sounds and feel of the environment.
- Use these real sensory experiences to enhance the realism of your visualisations.

10. Visualisation Variety Challenge:

- Each week, try a new variation of visualisation (e.g., slow-motion imagery, third-person perspective, future success scenario).
- Reflect on which techniques work best for you and incorporate them into your regular practice.

Remember, like any skill, visualisation improves with consistent practice. Be patient with yourself as you develop this mental skill, and don't hesitate to adjust these exercises to fit your personal preferences and schedule. With time and dedication, you'll find visualisation becoming a powerful tool in your padel performance arsenal.

In our next chapter, we'll explore the crucial topic of mental strategies during the game to help you control your emotions.

CHAPTER 7

IN-GAME MENTAL STRATEGIES

'The mind is everything. What you think, you become.' - Buddha

Padel is a dynamic sport and how you approach it mentally can be the x-factor that elevates your performance from good to great. This chapter explores some of the psychological strategies that will help you maintain composure, think strategically, and excel in various match situations.

1. Maintaining Emotional Control

Emotional mastery is the foundation of peak performance in padel. Let's look at several advanced techniques to help you stay composed and focused during intense matches.

Techniques for Staying Calm Under Pressure:

- Progressive Muscle Relaxation (PMR): This technique involves systematically tensing and relaxing different muscle groups. Between games, focus on tensing and relaxing your shoulders, arms, and hands to release physical tension. (Chapter 4)

- Mindfulness Micro-Practices: Develop the ability to center yourself quickly with short mindfulness exercises. For instance, during changeovers, practice a 30-second body scan, bringing awareness to each part of your body from toes to head.

- Anchor Words: Choose a word or phrase that instantly brings you back to a calm, focused state. This could be "steady," "flow," or any word that resonates with you. Use this anchor when you feel tension rising.

Managing Frustration and Anger:

- Cognitive Reframing: Train yourself to immediately reframe negative situations. If you miss a shot, instead of thinking "I'm playing terribly," shift to

"That's one thing I need to improve." Making mistakes in padel is a part of the game. Do not let one mistake define the rest.

of your game. It is one mistake, which means one point lost. Keeping focussed will reduce the number of mistakes going forward.

- Physical Reset: Develop a subtle physical gesture, like looking at your watch or adjusting your wristband, that serves as a trigger to reset your emotional state after a frustrating point.

- Controlled Expression: Instead of suppressing anger entirely, which can be counterproductive, learn to express it in a controlled, constructive manner. A firm but quiet "Come on!" can help release tension without losing composure.

Sustaining Positive Energy:

- Energy Matching: Pay attention to your partner's energy levels and consciously try to match and elevate them. This creates a positive feedback loop that can lift both players' performances.

- Micro-Celebrations: Develop subtle ways to celebrate small victories, even in tough matches. A quick fist pump or nod to your partner after a well-executed shot can maintain positivity.

- Gratitude Practice: During breaks, quickly list three things you're grateful for about the current match. This shifts your focus to the positive aspects of your experience.

2. Tactical Thinking and Decision Making

Elevating your mental game involves sharpening your tactical acumen and decision-making skills.

Reading the Game:

- Pattern Recognition Training: In practice, have your coach or partner deliberately create patterns in their play. Train yourself to spot these patterns quickly and anticipate the next move.

- Multi-Sensory Awareness: Beyond visual cues, train yourself to use auditory information. The sound of your opponent's racket on the ball can provide early information about the type and power of their shot.

- Opponent Profiling: Before matches, create mental profiles of your opponents if you've played them before. Note their tendencies, strengths, and weaknesses to inform your strategy.

Adapting Strategies Mid-Match:

- Tactical Timeouts: Learn to use official or unofficial breaks strategically. Use this time to reassess your approach and communicate adjustments with your partner.

- Flexibility Drills: In practice, set up scenarios where you must suddenly switch tactics mid-game. This improves your ability to adapt quickly in real match situations.

- Risk-Reward Analysis: Develop the skill of quickly assessing the risk and potential reward of different shot choices. Practice making these assessments in split seconds during drills.

Making Quick, Effective Decisions:

- Decision Trees: Create mental 'if-then' scenarios for common match situations. For example, "If opponent A is at the net and opponent B is deep, then I'll aim for a lob over A."

- Constraint-Based Learning: Practice with artificial constraints (e.g., only allowed to hit to certain areas of the court) to improve adaptive decision-making. This helps to build mental strength and gives you confidence in your technical ability.

- Pressure Testing: Regularly incorporate high-pressure scenarios in your practice sessions, like playing points where only the receiving team can score.

3. Mental Strategies for Different Game Situations

Different scorelines and match situations require tailored mental approaches.

Handling Leads:

- Momentum Maintenance: Develop strategies to maintain momentum when ahead. This might involve maintaining an aggressive playstyle or varying your tactics to keep opponents off-balance.

- Pressure Projection: Learn to subtly increase pressure on your opponent's when leading. This could involve taking slightly more time between points or displaying confident body language.

- Scenario Visualisation: Regularly visualise yourself successfully closing out matches from a leading position. This mental rehearsal builds confidence in your ability to maintain leads.

Coming from Behind:

- Milestone Setting: Break the comeback into smaller, achievable goals. For example, focus first on winning two points in a row, then a game, rather than the entire deficit.

- Energy Amplification: Consciously increase your positive energy when behind. This can disrupt your opponents' confidence and boost your own performance.

- Strategic Risk-Taking: Develop the courage to take calculated risks when trailing. This might involve more aggressive shot selection or tactical changes that can swing momentum.

Playing in Clutch Moments:

- Routine Reliance: Develop and stick to a consistent routine for high-pressure points. This familiarity can provide a sense of control in tense moments.

- Positive Trigger Words: Choose specific words or phrases to trigger a confident state in clutch moments. These should be practiced regularly so they become automatic in high-pressure situations.

- Breath Control: Master techniques like box breathing (inhale, hold, exhale, hold, each for equal counts) to regulate your physiological response in tense moments.

RECAP AND ACTION ITEMS

You've now explored a comprehensive set of advanced mental strategies for in-game performance. Here are expanded action steps to integrate these into your padel practice:

1. Emotional Regulation:

- Take a few minutes to reflect on your emotional states during matches.

- Note triggers, responses, and the effectiveness of different regulation techniques.

- Review weekly to identify patterns and areas for improvement.

2. Tactical Analysis Project:

- Record and analyse your matches, if you are able to, focusing on decision-making moments.

- Log one important decision into your mental journal, noting why you made it and its positive outcome.

- Develop a mental playbook of effective tactics for different opponents and situations.

3. Pressure Simulation Program:

- Work with your coach to design a progressive program of pressure-inducing drills.

- Start with mild pressure situations and gradually increase intensity over time.

- Track your performance and comfort level in these drills to measure improvement.

4. Mindfulness and Concentration Training:

- Commit to a daily mindfulness practice, starting with 5 minutes and increasing over time.

- Use apps or guided sessions to explore different mindfulness techniques.

- Integrate short mindfulness exercises into your on-court training routine.

5. Scenario-Based Mental Rehearsal:

- Spend 10 minutes daily visualising yourself successfully handling various match scenarios.

- Create detailed, multi-sensory mental images of performing well in challenging situations.

- Gradually increase the complexity and pressure of the scenarios you visualise.

By consistently applying and refining these advanced mental strategies, you'll develop a psychological edge that complements your physical skills. Remember, mental toughness is a skill that can be developed with practice and patience. Embrace the process of mental training and watch as your overall game improves on the padel court.

In our next chapter, we'll explore techniques for managing performance anxiety, building on the emotional control and mental strategies we've covered here. Get ready to transform pre-match nerves into a powerful tool for enhanced performance.

CHAPTER 8

OVERCOMING PERFORMANCE ANXIETY

'Everything you have ever wanted is sitting on the other side of fear.' - George Addair

When you step onto the padel court, the flutter in your chest isn't just from physical exertion. It's the anticipation, the excitement, and sometimes, the nerve-wracking anxiety that can grip even the most seasoned players. Performance anxiety isn't just a stray thought; it's a complex beast that can affect your game in ways you might not even realise. Let's break it down and explore how to tame this beast.

Understanding Performance Anxiety in Padel

Symptoms and Triggers:

Knowing the symptoms of performance anxiety can help you recognise it in its nascent stages. Physically, you might notice your heart racing, palms sweating, or muscles tensing unusually. Mentally, you might find yourself plagued by a barrage of self-doubt or catastrophic predictions.

Common triggers include the fear of disappointing teammates, the pressure of competition, or even the presence of a particularly critical audience. Identifying your personal triggers is crucial; it's like mapping the minefield so you can navigate through it more safely.

Impact on Play:

Anxiety can hijack your attention, diverting your mental resources away from where they're needed most. This mental distraction is a recipe for mistakes and can make you play more conservatively than you normally would. It can also mess with your physical performance, causing muscle tension, slower reaction times, and quicker fatigue.

Common Anxiety-Inducing Situations:

Recognising common anxiety-inducing situations in padel can empower you to prepare more effectively. These might include playing in highly competitive matches, facing an opponent who has previously beaten you, or performing in front of a large crowd. Even internal team dynamics, like playing with a new partner or stepping into a leadership role, can stir up anxiety.

Anxiety Reduction Strategies:

When it comes to taming the jittery beast of performance anxiety, having a toolkit of strategies can be very helpful in managing these anxiety feelings. Here are some effective methods to help you keep your cool on the court.

Controlled Breathing Techniques:

Mastering controlled breathing can help flip the script, turning what could be a panic trigger into a calming lifeline. Try the 4-7-8 technique: Inhale slowly through your nose for a count of four, hold that breath for a count of seven, then exhale completely through your mouth for a count of eight. Practice this regularly to make it second nature when you need it most.

Progressive Muscle Relaxation:

Progressive muscle relaxation (PMR) involves tensing and then relaxing different muscle groups in your body. Start at your feet and work your way up, tensing each muscle group for about five seconds and then relaxing for 30 seconds. Pay attention to the contrast between the tension and the relaxation. This technique can be incredibly soothing and help you release muscle tension right there on the spot. (Detailed in Chapter 4)

Cognitive Behavioural Techniques:

Cognitive behavioural techniques (CBT) are all about identifying and changing the thought patterns that contribute to your anxiety. Start by observing your thoughts during a match. Are they helpful or hurtful? Once you identify a common negative thought, try to counter it with a positive or realistic one. Replace "I always miss these shots" with "I am going to make the next one."

Visualisation:

Another powerful CBT tool is visualisation. Before a match, spend a few minutes closing your eyes and imagining yourself playing confidently and successfully. This not only boosts your mood but also primes your mind for success. (Refer to Chapter 6)

Transforming Anxiety into Excitement

Anxiety doesn't have to be your adversary. Instead, think of it as a misunderstood ally. What if you could harness that surge of adrenaline to elevate your game in padel?

Reappraisal Techniques:

The skill of cognitive reappraisal involves changing your emotional response to a situation by reinterpreting its meaning. When you catch yourself thinking, "I'm nervous about this match," pause and rephrase it to, "I'm excited about this opportunity to challenge myself." This slight shift in vocabulary can profoundly influence your emotional and physiological responses.

Embracing Nervous Energy:

Nervous energy is a resource, not a curse. It's your body gearing up, getting you ready to face a challenge head-on. Embrace it. Use it to sharpen your focus and reflexes. Channel it into your shots, your runs, and your tactical thinking. Say to yourself, "This is my body preparing me to perform at my best."

Pre-performance Routines:

Establishing a pre-performance routine is like setting the stage for a play. It's about creating a familiar and comforting sequence of actions that you perform before every game. Your routine could involve listening to a specific playlist, a series of stretches followed by visualisation techniques, or a particular sequence of warm-up hits with your partner. Whatever it is, make it consistent. The key is to develop a set of actions that automatically puts you in 'game mode' and signals to your body and mind that it's time to perform.

By integrating these techniques, you're not just managing anxiety; you're actively converting it into an asset. Anxiety no longer becomes something to dread or combat, but a vital component of your success on the padel court. Harness it correctly and watch as it propels you towards levels of performance you might have thought were out of reach. Embrace the flutter, channel the surge, and transform the jitters into jubilation. Let your anxiety work for you, driving you forward, not holding you back.

Remember, the goal isn't to eliminate anxiety completely; it's to understand it, manage it, and use it to your advantage. With practice and persistence, you'll not only elevate your performance on the court but you will also enjoy the game more, which, after all, is what playing padel should be all about.

RECAP AND ACTION ITEMS

We looked at the complexities of performance anxiety in padel, explaining its symptoms, triggers, and detrimental effects on gameplay. This chapter highlights the importance of recognising anxiety's impact on both physical and mental performance. The chapter then introduces practical strategies to manage anxiety, including breathing techniques, muscle relaxation, cognitive behavioural techniques, and reappraisal methods. It emphasises transforming anxiety into a positive force by harnessing nervous energy and establishing pre-performance routines. Ultimately, the aim of this chapter is to promote a mindset shift, encouraging you to view anxiety as a potential asset rather than an obstacle.

1. Identify personal anxiety triggers:

- Reflect on past experiences to pinpoint specific situations that induce anxiety, and then use the techniques discussed to change this way of thinking.

2. Practice breathing and relaxation techniques:

- Incorporate controlled breathing and progressive muscle relaxation into daily routines for familiarity under pressure.

3. Challenge negative thoughts:

- Develop a habit of counteracting negative self-talk with positive affirmations.

4. **Visualise success:**

- Regularly engage in mental imagery to envision confident and successful performances.

5. **Create a pre-performance routine:**

- Design a consistent set of actions to prepare mentally and physically for matches.

6. **Reappraise anxiety as excitement:**

- Practice reframing anxious thoughts into positive and energising ones.

7. **Embrace nervous energy:**

- Channel adrenaline into focused and powerful gameplay.

By consistently applying these action items, you will learn to effectively manage performance anxiety and unlock your full potential on the padel court.

CHAPTER 9

DEALING WITH MISTAKES AND SETBACKS

'Success is not final, failure is not fatal: It is the courage to continue that counts.' - Winston Churchill

Developing a Healthy Perspective on Errors

Mistakes on the padel court aren't just inevitable; they're an essential part of your growth as a player. How you perceive and handle these errors can significantly influence your overall game and your enjoyment of this fast-paced sport. Let's look at how transforming your view on mistakes can pave the way for improvement, resilience, and ultimately, greater success in padel.

Learning from Mistakes

Every error you make on the court holds valuable lessons. The trick is to shift your focus from frustration to analysis. After a missed shot or a lost point, instead of getting caught up in a whirlwind of self-criticism, ask yourself, "What can I learn from this?" This approach not only alleviates the sting of the mistake but also sets you up for better performance in future games.

For instance, if you notice you've hit several backhand shots into the net, consider the technique you're using. Are you keeping your eye on the ball until the moment of impact? Are your feet positioned correctly? Reflecting on these questions can reveal adjustments that may significantly elevate your game.

After each game, take a few minutes to think about which shot you were executing badly. Then at your next practice, work on this until you regain your confidence. Remember, the goal here isn't to dwell on what went wrong but to use each game as a stepping stone towards becoming a more skilled player.

Accepting Imperfection

Padel, like any sport, is a journey of continuous learning, and perfection is an impossible and frankly, a rather dull destination. Imagine if we all played padel with total perfection, when would a game end? It would be great if we could achieve this however, it is unrealistic in any sport to accomplish this. Embracing imperfection is about understanding and accepting that mistakes are part of the game and part of being human. This acceptance will not only reduce the pressure you put on yourself but also enhance your ability to enjoy playing, regardless of the outcome.

Think of the world's top athletes; they all make mistakes. However, they don't let these moments define their entire performance or career. Instead, they accept them as part of the process and move on. You should, too. Next time you step onto the court, give yourself the freedom to play without the weight of needing to be perfect. You'll likely find that this mindset not only reduces anxiety but also improves your performance, as you're playing more freely and with greater focus on the game itself, rather than on avoiding errors.

The Role of Mistakes in Improvement

Understanding the role mistakes play in your development as a player is crucial. Every error provides a unique opportunity for growth. It's a feedback loop that, if listened to, can significantly accelerate your learning curve. The key is to see mistakes as constructive feedback, not as a reflection of your abilities as a player.

This perspective encourages a proactive approach to improvement. For example, if you frequently find yourself out of position, instead of berating yourself, use this as a cue to work on your spatial awareness and communication with your partner. Perhaps, spend additional time practicing these aspects or discuss strategies with more experienced players or coaches.

Additionally, this mindset can lead to innovation in your playing style. Sometimes, the best techniques are born from the ashes of a spectacular failure. By experimenting with different strategies and being open to the outcomes, you're more likely to develop unique skills that can set you apart from your competitors.

In-Match Error Management and Quick Recovery Techniques

So, you've just made a mistake in the middle of a padel match. What now? The ball has sailed past you, or worse, into the net, and that sinking feeling is starting to set in. Here's your first tool in the toolbox: quick recovery techniques. First off, it's about the physical reset, then the mental.

Take a breath. Not just any breath, but a deep, diaphragmatic breath. This type of breathing not only helps to calm your nervous system but also resets your focus. Think of it as hitting the refresh button on your computer. Just as you wouldn't expect your tech to work without a reboot now and then, your body and mind are the same.

Next, have a short, specific routine after points. Rafael Nadal has his meticulous bottle alignment and specific on-court movements; these aren't just quirks but deliberate techniques to regain control and composure. For you, it could be as simple as adjusting your grip, tapping your racket twice against your shoe, or walking back to the service line with a particular thought in mind. This routine acts as a psychological signal that the last point is over, and it's time to focus on the next.

Maintaining Composure After Errors

Now, let's address the heart rate and the heat of the moment—maintaining your composure. Padel, like life, throws curveballs, and how you react can make all the difference. The key here is not to suppress your disappointment—acknowledge it, but don't let it dictate your next move.

One technique is the 10-second rule. Give yourself 10 seconds of internal dialogue to express frustration, analyse briefly what went wrong, then switch gears. You could say to yourself, "Okay, that was a bad shot because I rushed. Slow it down next point." This quick self-talk helps to prevent the buildup of frustration and keeps the negative emotions from spiralling.

Next vital component is body language. Keep your head up, shoulders back, and maintain a confident posture. Body language not only influences how you feel but also how your opponent perceives you. A defeated posture can be like a shark smelling blood in the water; it gives your opponent a psychological edge.

Refocusing Strategies

You've acknowledged the mistake, you've kept your cool, now it's time to refocus. This final piece is crucial because an unfocused player is often an unsuccessful one. Refocusing is about bringing your mind back to the present — not the last point, not the next game, but this moment, right here.

One effective method is to use focal points. These could be physical objects or specific thoughts. For instance, focus on the texture of the grip tape, the sound of the ball hitting the racket, or the pattern of your breath. These focal points act as anchors, keeping your mind tethered to the present and not drifting back to past errors or forward to uncertain outcomes.

Another strategy involves setting small, immediate goals. Instead of worrying about winning the set or match, focus on winning the next point or even just making a good return. Breaking down the game into smaller, manageable pieces helps to keep the pressure manageable and your mind engaged.

Long-Term Resilience Building

Post-Match Analysis

Every match, whether a win or a loss, is packed with valuable lessons, waiting to be unearthed by a discerning eye. The process of post-match analysis is crucial in developing your long-term resilience because it allows you to step back and objectively assess your performance. Begin by reviewing the match as soon as possible after its conclusion. This could be through watching video recordings or simply sitting down and going through the game in your mind. Identify key moments where a mistake was made, or a setback occurred. What led up to those moments? Could anything have been done differently? Do not dwell on this but rather use this as a tool for learning.

Analyse your decision-making, shot selection, movement, and tactical awareness. It's not just about identifying what went wrong but also recognising what went right. This balanced view prevents the analysis from becoming a self-critique session and instead turns it into a constructive learning experience.

Developing a Growth Mindset

As mentioned before, the concept of a growth mindset, introduced by psychologist Carol Dweck, is based on the belief that your basic qualities are things you can cultivate through your efforts. When it comes to padel, adopting a growth mindset means understanding that your abilities in serving, volleying, or strategy aren't fixed but can be improved with persistence and hard work.

Translate this mindset into your training and match play. For instance, if you find yourself struggling with backhand shots, instead of thinking, "I'm just not good at backhands," consider what specific aspects of the backhand you can improve. Is it the grip, the swing, or the positioning? With this mindset, every error becomes a pointer to a specific area that can be developed.

Building Self-Compassion

While cultivating a rigorous spirit and a relentless pursuit of improvement are important, it's equally crucial to learn to be kind to yourself. Self-compassion in sports is about acknowledging that making mistakes is part of learning and growing. It's about treating yourself with the same kindness and understanding that you would offer a teammate who missed a crucial shot.

Start by recognising the harsh self-talk that often accompanies errors. Replace thoughts like "I'm such a terrible player" with "Everyone makes mistakes, I can learn from this." It's about understanding that one bad game doesn't define your ability or your worth as a player. Practicing mindfulness can be a useful tool in building self-compassion. Techniques such as focused breathing or meditation can help you manage the emotions that come with playing padel. They allow you to maintain a calm, present state of mind, which is crucial not only for managing stress during matches but also for reflecting on your performance afterward without being overly critical.

By integrating these practices into your routine—regularly analysing your performances, fostering a growth mindset, and treating yourself with compassion—you lay the groundwork for not just recovering from setbacks but using them as catalysts for growth. This holistic approach to resilience ensures that you're not only getting better at the game of padel but also constantly evolving as a competitor and individual.

RECAP AND ACTION ITEMS

This chapter explores the importance of a positive mindset when dealing with mistakes in padel. It emphasises the value of learning from errors, accepting imperfection, and understanding the role of mistakes in improvement. The chapter also provides practical strategies for managing errors during matches, including quick recovery techniques, maintaining composure, and refocusing. Lastly, it highlights the significance of long-term resilience building through post-match analysis, developing a growth mindset, and practicing self-compassion.

1. **Embrace mistakes as learning opportunities:**

- View errors as valuable feedback for improvement. Do not dwell on errors but rather use them to implement change and the opportunity to improve.

2. **Develop a post-match analysis routine:**

   - Regularly review matches to identify strengths and areas for growth.

3. **Practice quick recovery techniques:**

   - Implement breathing and mental reset strategies after mistakes.

4. **Cultivate a growth mindset:**

   - Believe in your ability to improve through effort and practice.

5. **Build self-compassion:**

   - Treat yourself with kindness and understanding when making mistakes.

6. **Set realistic goals:**

- Focus on small, achievable goals during matches to reduce pressure.

7. **Develop a mental routine:**

- Create a consistent routine to regain focus after errors.

8. **Practice mindfulness:**

- Incorporate mindfulness techniques to manage emotions and stay present.

CHAPTER 10

WORKING WITH YOUR PARTNER

'Alone we can do so little; together we can do so much.'
- Helen Keller

This final chapter is, without doubt, one of the most critical in your journey to padel mastery. While individual skill is important, it's the ability to function as a cohesive unit that truly sets apart the champions in this sport. Padel, at its core, is a game of partnerships.

You might possess the most powerful smash, the most precise volley, or the craftiest lob in the world. However, these individual skills, impressive as they may be, pale in comparison to the strength of a synchronised team. True success in padel comes from the ability to think, play, and react as one unified force on the court.

As we discuss this topic, you'll discover that effective communication is indeed invaluable. Beyond that, we'll explore something even more profound: the intuitive understanding between partners that elevates the game to an art form. There's an indescribable satisfaction in knowing exactly where your partner will be on the court without even looking. It's that moment when you can confidently leave a shot, trusting that your teammate will cover it. It's the instinctive knowledge of when to play the ball to support your partner, even before they call for it.

This level of synergy doesn't happen by chance. It's cultivated through dedicated practice, open communication, and a deep commitment to your partnership. As you progress through this chapter, you'll learn strategies to develop this sixth sense with your partner, transforming your duo from two individuals into a seamless team.

Remember, in padel, the whole is always greater than the sum of its parts. Two players who understand this principle and work tirelessly to embody it will consistently triumph over more individually skilled opponents who lack this cohesion.

1. Effective On-Court Communication

This is one of the most important factors of improving your game. It's not just about calling shots or signalling moves; it's an intricate dance of verbal and non-verbal cues, positive reinforcement, and constructive feedback that can make or break your performance as a team.

Verbal and Non-verbal Cues:

Communication on the padel court transcends spoken words. It encompasses a range of signals — a subtle nod, a quick glance, a deliberate gesture — each loaded with meaning. These cues form a silent language that, when fluently spoken between partners, can not only intimidate opponents but also control the flow of the game.

Key aspects of verbal and non-verbal cues:

- Pre-match Signal Establishment: Before stepping onto the court, take time to establish a set of simple, clear signals with your partner. These could range from hand gestures indicating "I'm taking this shot" to specific looks that mean "cover the backcourt."

- Consistency in Signalling: The power of these cues lies in their consistency. Use them reliably to avoid confusion during critical points.

- Verbal Call Efficiency: Employ short, sharp verbal calls like "yours," "mine," "leave," or "go." These should be loud enough to be heard but not so forceful as to startle your partner.

- Evolving Communication: As your partnership develops, your cues can become more nuanced. A flick of the wrist or a quick glance might be all you need to communicate complex strategies mid-play.

Techniques for improving on-court communication:

- Dedicated Signal Practice: Incorporate specific practice sessions focused solely on developing and refining your cue system.

- Scenario-based Role-playing: Simulate various match scenarios to practice using your cues under different pressures and situations.

- Regular Communication Audits: Schedule regular debriefs with your partner to discuss the effectiveness of your current communication strategy and areas for improvement.

- Silent Drills: Practice playing points or even entire practice sets using only non-verbal cues to strengthen your silent communication skills.

Positive Reinforcement:

The heat of the game can bring out intense emotions, but the best players know how to channel this intensity through positive reinforcement. Celebrating small victories, such as a well-placed shot or a game won, can significantly boost morale and maintain energy levels throughout the match.

Impact of positive reinforcement:

- Confidence Building: Acknowledging your partner's good plays boosts their self-assurance and encourages repeat performances.

- Behaviour Reinforcement: Positive feedback reinforces the behaviours and strategies you want to see more often in your partner's play.

- Partnership Strengthening: Regular positive interactions strengthen the bond between partners, creating a more cohesive team.

- Momentum Maintenance: Positive reinforcement can help maintain momentum during a match, even when facing challenges.

Techniques for effective positive reinforcement:

- Physical Affirmations: Use high-fives, fist bumps, or supportive pats on the back after good plays.

- Verbal Encouragement: Employ encouraging phrases like "great shot," "nice recovery," or "excellent read" to acknowledge good play.

- Positive Body Language: Maintain an open, energetic posture even after errors to show continued support and confidence.

- Constructive Responses to Errors: React to mistakes with encouraging phrases like "no worries, let's get the next one" to maintain a positive atmosphere.

Constructive Feedback:

Feedback, when given constructively, can transform a good padel partnership into a great one. The key is to ensure that your criticisms are productive and aimed at improving your joint performance, not assigning blame.

Key aspects of constructive feedback:

- Action-Focused Critique: Focus on specific actions and outcomes rather than personal critiques. Instead of "You're not hitting well today," try "I've noticed your shots are going a bit long, maybe try adjusting your swing?"

- Timing Consideration: Choose appropriate moments for detailed feedback. During a match might not always be ideal; consider saving extensive critiques for practice sessions or post-match discussions.

- Collaborative Approach: Combine feedback with questions to promote problem-solving together. For example, "I think we're getting crowded at the net. How do you feel about spacing out a bit more?"

Techniques for providing constructive feedback:

- "I" Statement Usage: Frame feedback using "I" statements to avoid sounding accusatory. For instance, "I feel we could improve our net coverage" rather than "You're not covering the net well."

- Specific Behaviour Focus: Offer feedback on specific, observable behaviours rather than general criticisms.

- Solution-Oriented Approach: Always pair critiques with suggestions for improvement or invite your partner to brainstorm solutions together.

- Feedback Sandwiching: When possible, start with a positive observation, then provide the constructive criticism, and end with another positive point or an encouraging statement about future improvement.

2. Building Strong Partnerships

Understanding Partner Dynamics:

Every player brings their unique style, strengths, and personality to the court. Recognising and adapting to these individual dynamics can be the cornerstone of your success as a doubles team.

Key aspects of partner dynamics:

- Playing Styles: Understand if your partner tends to be aggressive, defensive, or somewhere in between. Do they thrive on long rallies or prefer quick, decisive points?

- Stress Responses: Observe how your partner reacts under pressure. Do they become more focused or tend to make rash decisions?

- Communication Preferences: Some players prefer constant verbal interaction, while others might favour minimal talk and more non-verbal cues.

- Decision-making Tendencies: Notice whether your partner is more instinctive or analytical in their approach to the game.

Techniques for improving partner understanding:

- Regular Strategy Sessions: Schedule time outside of matches to discuss preferred strategies, playstyles, and match approaches.

- Situational Observation: Pay close attention to your partner's performance under different circumstances – when leading, when behind, or in high-pressure situations.

- Varied Scenario Practice: Incorporate a wide range of match scenarios in your practice sessions to gauge each other's reactions and adaptability.

- Personal History Sharing: Take time to understand each other's padel journey, including past experiences, significant wins or losses, and personal goals in the sport.

Developing Trust and Rapport:

Trust forms the foundation of any successful padel team. It extends beyond believing in your partner's shot-making abilities; it's about creating a supportive environment where both players feel valued and confident.

Key elements of trust and rapport:

- Off-court Relationship Building: Spending time together outside of padel can significantly enhance your on-court chemistry.

- Consistent On-court Support: Demonstrating unwavering support during matches, especially after mistakes or during challenging moments.

- Open Communication Channels: Fostering an environment where both partners feel comfortable sharing thoughts, concerns, and ideas about the game.

- Shared Responsibility: Embracing both victories and defeats as a team, avoiding blame and focusing on collective growth.

Techniques for building trust:

- Regular Team-building Activities: Engage in activities outside of padel that require teamwork and communication.

- Post-match Debriefs: Implement a routine of honest, constructive discussions after each match or practice session.

- Trust-building Exercises: Incorporate specific drills or exercises in your practice that require reliance on your partner.

- Vulnerability Sharing: Create opportunities to share fears, weaknesses, or areas of insecurity related to your game, fostering a deeper understanding and support between partners.

Complementing Each Other's Strengths:

A savvy doubles team knows how to leverage their individual strengths and compensate for each other's weaknesses, creating a synergy that's greater than the sum of its parts.

Strategies for complementing strengths:

- Comprehensive Skill Assessment: Regularly evaluate both players' skills through structured practice sessions and match analysis.

- Tailored Game Plans: Develop strategies that highlight each partner's strengths while minimising exposure of weaknesses.

- Adaptive Positioning: Adjust court positioning to maximise coverage based on each player's strengths and mobility.

- Role Definition: Clearly define roles within the partnership based on individual strengths but remain flexible to adapt as needed.

Techniques for strength optimization:

- Strength-Weakness Mapping: Create a detailed map of both players' strengths and weaknesses, updating it regularly.

- Pre-match Strategy Sessions: Before each match, discuss how to best utilise your combined strengths against specific opponents.

- In-game Flexibility: Develop signals or short phrases to quickly adjust tactics based on the effectiveness of your strategy during a match.

- Cross-training: Work on improving each other's weaker areas during practice to create a more well-rounded team.

3. Conflict Resolution in Doubles

Addressing Disagreements Constructively:

Conflict is inevitable in any dynamic partnership. The key to success lies not in avoiding disagreements but in handling them constructively and using them as opportunities for growth.

Key principles of constructive conflict resolution:

- Issue-Centric Approach: Focus discussions on specific issues or behaviours rather than personal criticisms.

- Timely Addressing: Deal with conflicts promptly to prevent the build-up of resentment or misunderstandings.

- Active Listening: Make a conscious effort to understand your partner's perspective fully before responding.

- Solution Orientation: Approach conflicts with a mindset focused on finding mutually beneficial solutions.

Techniques for constructive conflict resolution:

- "I" Statement Utilisation: Frame your concerns using "I" statements to express your feelings without sounding accusatory. For example, "I feel unsure about our net strategy" instead of "You're not coming to the net consistently."

- Timeout Requests: Establish a system where either partner can call a brief timeout during a match to address immediate concerns or realign strategies.

- Reflective Listening Practice: Implement the technique of repeating back what you've heard to ensure clear understanding and show that you value your partner's input.

- Written Communication: For more complex issues, consider writing down your thoughts to organise them clearly before discussing with your partner.

Managing Emotions During Conflicts:

Emotional management is crucial not only for resolving conflicts effectively but also for maintaining performance levels during a match. Learning to regulate your emotions can be the difference between a minor setback and a match-losing meltdown.

Key aspects of emotional management:

- Self-awareness: Develop the ability to recognise your own emotional state and its potential impact on your game.

- Body Language Control: Understand the power of non-verbal communication and maintain composed body language even when feeling frustrated.

- Shared Goal Focus: Remind yourself and your partner of your shared objectives to help maintain perspective during heated moments.

- Emotional Contagion Awareness: Recognise how your emotional state can affect your partner and vice versa.

Techniques for emotion management:

- Breathing Exercises: Practice deep breathing techniques that you can use during matches to calm yourself.

- Positive Self-talk: Develop a set of positive affirmations or mantras to use when feeling overwhelmed or frustrated.

- Visualisation: Use mental imagery techniques to picture yourself responding calmly and effectively to stressful situations.

- Emotional Check-ins: Implement regular emotional check-ins with your partner during matches to ensure you're both in a good headspace.

Strategies for Realignment During Matches:

Even the strongest partnerships can be thrown off their game by conflicts or external pressures. Having strategies for quick realignment is crucial for maintaining performance and team cohesion.

Key realignment strategies:

- Reset Routine Development: Create a specific routine or ritual that signals a fresh start for both partners.

- Mini-goal Setting: Break down the remainder of the match into smaller, more manageable objectives to regain focus and motivation.

- Open Communication Maintenance: Keep dialogue open throughout the match, regularly checking in on tactics, energy levels, and emotional states.

- Flexibility in Roles: Be prepared to adjust your usual roles or strategies if your current approach isn't working.

Techniques for effective realignment:

- Physical Reset Cue: Develop a specific physical gesture, like a unique handshake or fist bump, to serve as a 'reset button' for your team.

- Tactical Timeouts: Use official timeouts strategically to reassess your game plan and realign your mindset.

- Positive Memory Recall: Remind each other of past successes or strong performances to boost confidence and refocus on your strengths.

- Partner-specific Motivation: Develop personalised ways to motivate and re-energize your partner based on their individual preferences and responses.

RECAP AND ACTION ITEMS

Mastering communication and teamwork in doubles padel is a complex but rewarding journey. It requires a deep understanding of both verbal and non-verbal communication, the ability to provide and receive constructive feedback, and the skills to build a strong, trusting partnership. Moreover, it involves developing strategies for conflict resolution and emotional management that can keep your team cohesive and performing at its best, even under pressure.

1. Communication Audit:

- Implement a routine of brief, post-match discussions to evaluate the effectiveness of your communication, partnership dynamics, and any conflicts that arose. Use a structured format to ensure you cover all aspects consistently.

2. Cue System Development:

- During your next training session, work with your partner to develop and practice a comprehensive system of verbal and non-verbal cues. Start with basic signals and gradually introduce more nuanced cues as you become comfortable.

3. Team Bonding Activity:

- Plan a non-padel related activity with your partner to strengthen your personal rapport. This could be anything from a casual lunch to an escape room challenge that requires teamwork.

4. Conflict Resolution Practice:

- In your next practice session, simulate a disagreement scenario and apply the conflict resolution techniques discussed. Take turns initiating the conflict to practice from both perspectives.

5. Reset Routine Creation:

- Develop a 'reset routine' with your partner to use during matches when you need to realign. Practice this routine regularly so it becomes second nature when you need it most.

6. Emotional Management Techniques:

- Each partner should identify their preferred emotional management technique (e.g., deep breathing, visualisation) and practice it daily. Share these techniques with each other so you can provide appropriate support during matches.

7. Strength-Weakness Analysis:

- Conduct a thorough analysis of both partners' strengths and weaknesses. Use this to create a strategy map that outlines how you'll leverage your strengths and cover for each other's weaknesses in different match scenarios.

By diligently integrating these practices into your routine, you'll not only enhance your performance but also cultivate a more rewarding and resilient partnership on the padel court. Remember, effective teamwork is the secret ingredient that can transform good players into a formidable, championship-calibre team. Embrace the journey of growth together, and watch as your communication, trust, and performance reach new heights.

As you close this book, consider it not as the end but as a launching pad for your continued success. The concepts and strategies discussed are seeds that, when nurtured by practice and perseverance, will flourish into extraordinary achievements. Keep pushing your limits, challenging your boundaries, and pursuing excellence. The world of padel awaits your unique imprint, and beyond it, a multitude of arenas where you can demonstrate the power of a winning mindset.

Printed by Amazon Italia Logistica S.r.l.
Torrazza Piemonte (TO), Italy

64449111R00094